Q. What do you call a man that co

Q. What did the house wear to a party?

Q. Why is Peter Pan flying all the time?

Q. Why do celebrities always keep their cool?

Q. What's the best nation in the world?

A) Donation! Can you give me $10?

Q. What is a parents favourite carol?

A) Silent night!

Q. Is this pool safe for diving?

Q. What did the drummer call his twin daughter?

Q. What nut doesn't like money?

Q. Where do you learn to make ice cream?

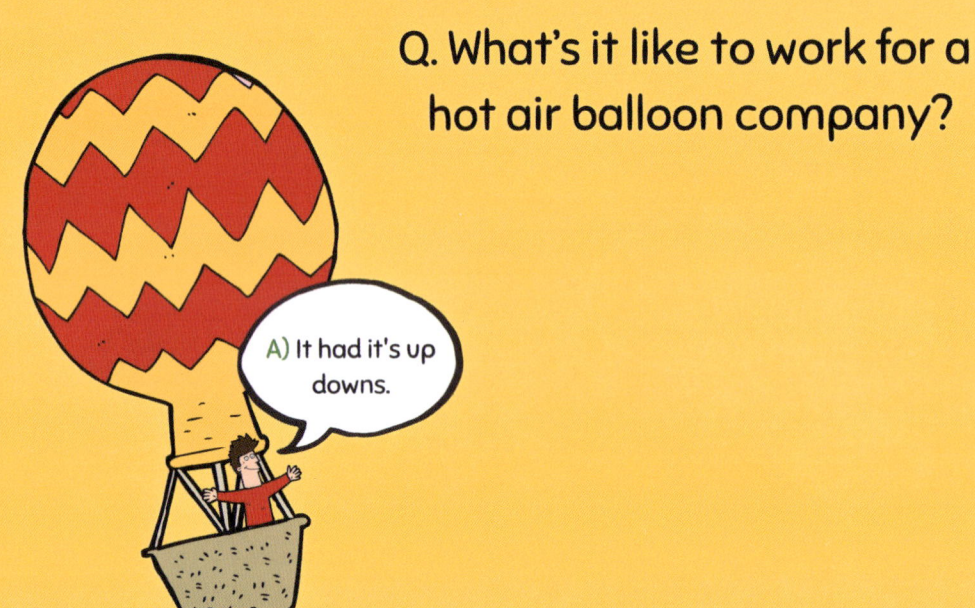

Q. What did the paper say to the pencil?

Q. What do you call an alligator in a vest?

Q. Who is the world's greatest underwater secret agent?

Q. What do you call a guy lying on your doorstep?

Q. What do elves learn at school?

Q. What do you call a fairy that doesn't like to shower?

Q. What do you call a blind dinosaur?

Q. What do you do if you see a spaceman?

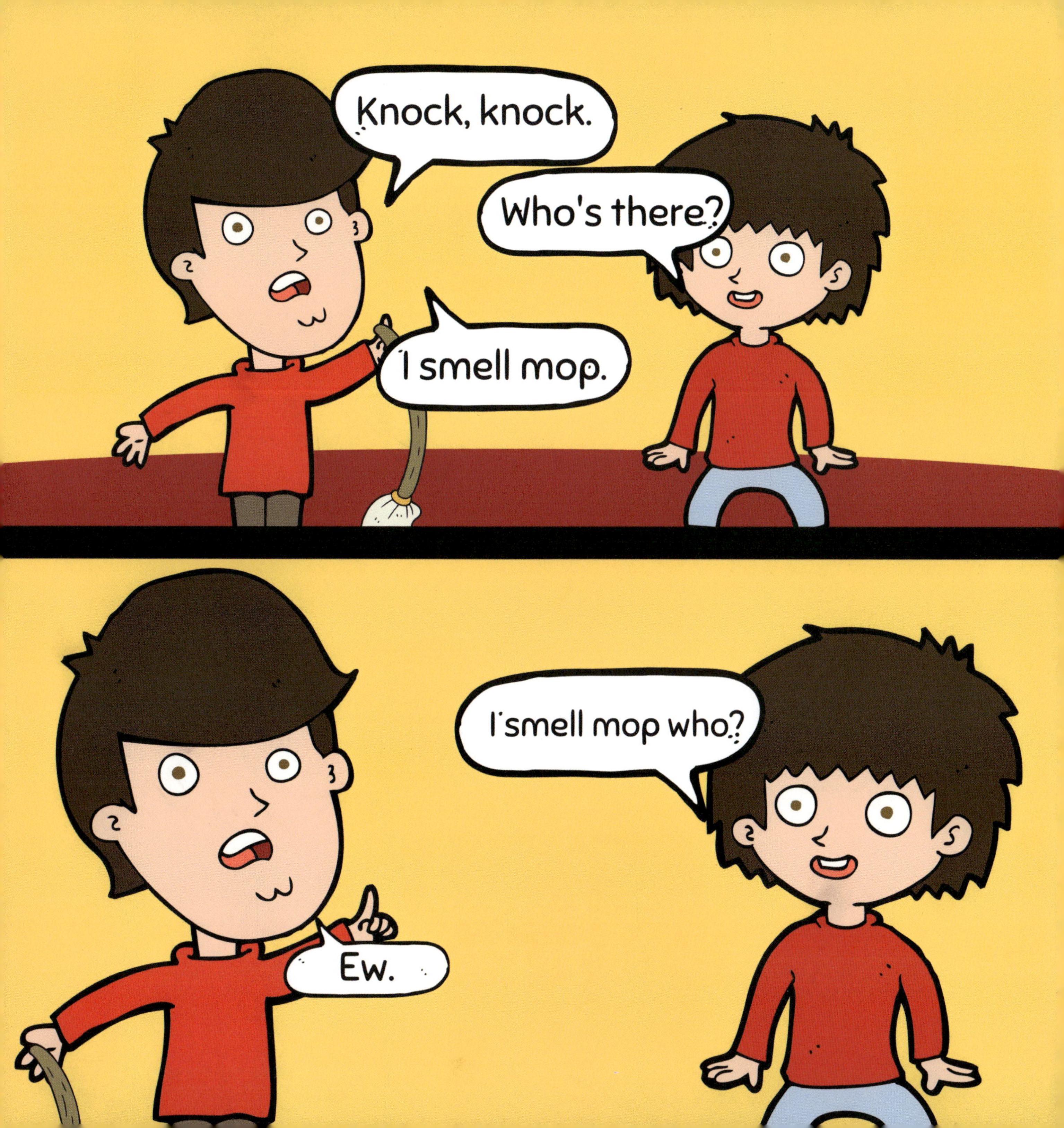
Knock, knock.
Who's there?
I smell mop.
I smell mop who?
Ew.

Q. What do lazy farmers grow?

Q. What did one ocean say to the other?

Q. Why did the picture go to jail?

A) Because it was framed!

I used to have a job collecting leaves.

I was raking it in!

Q. How does a penguin build its house?

Q. What did the police officer say to the belly button?

What does a lemon say when it answers the phone?

Q. How do you make a tissue dance?

Q. Why is a doctor always so calm?

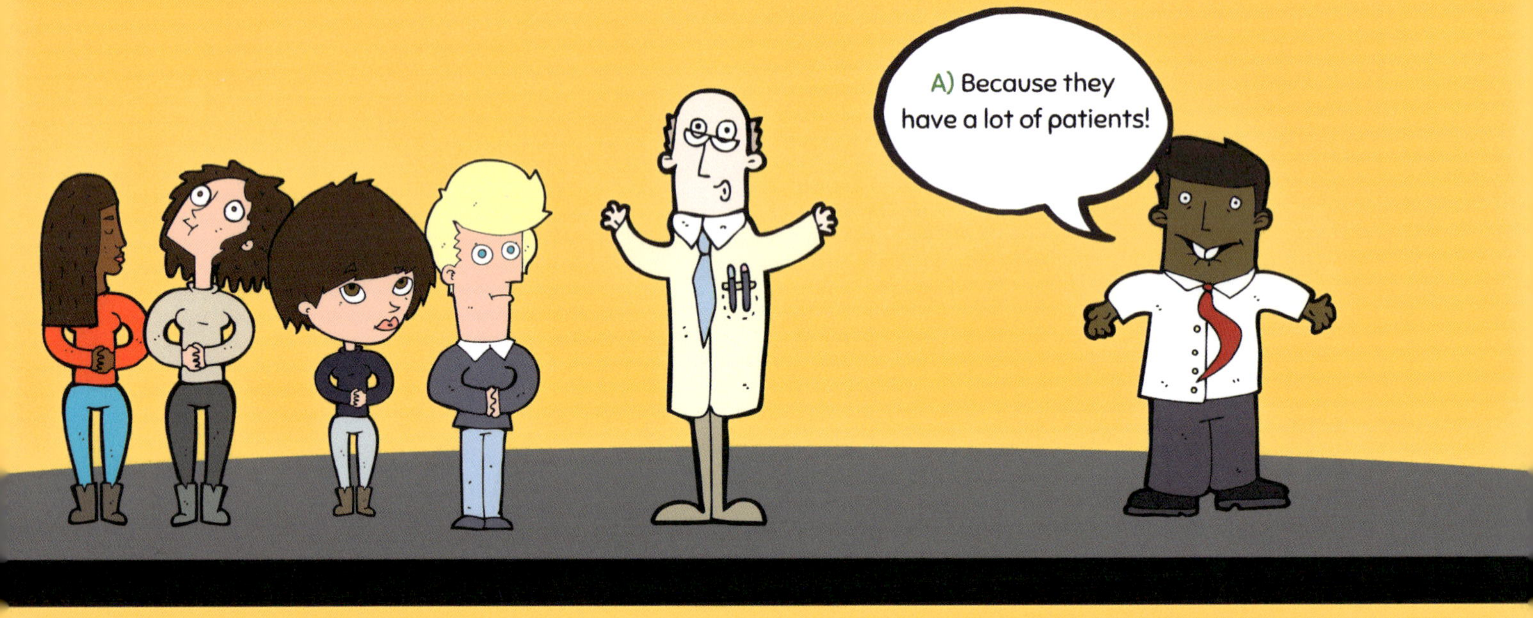

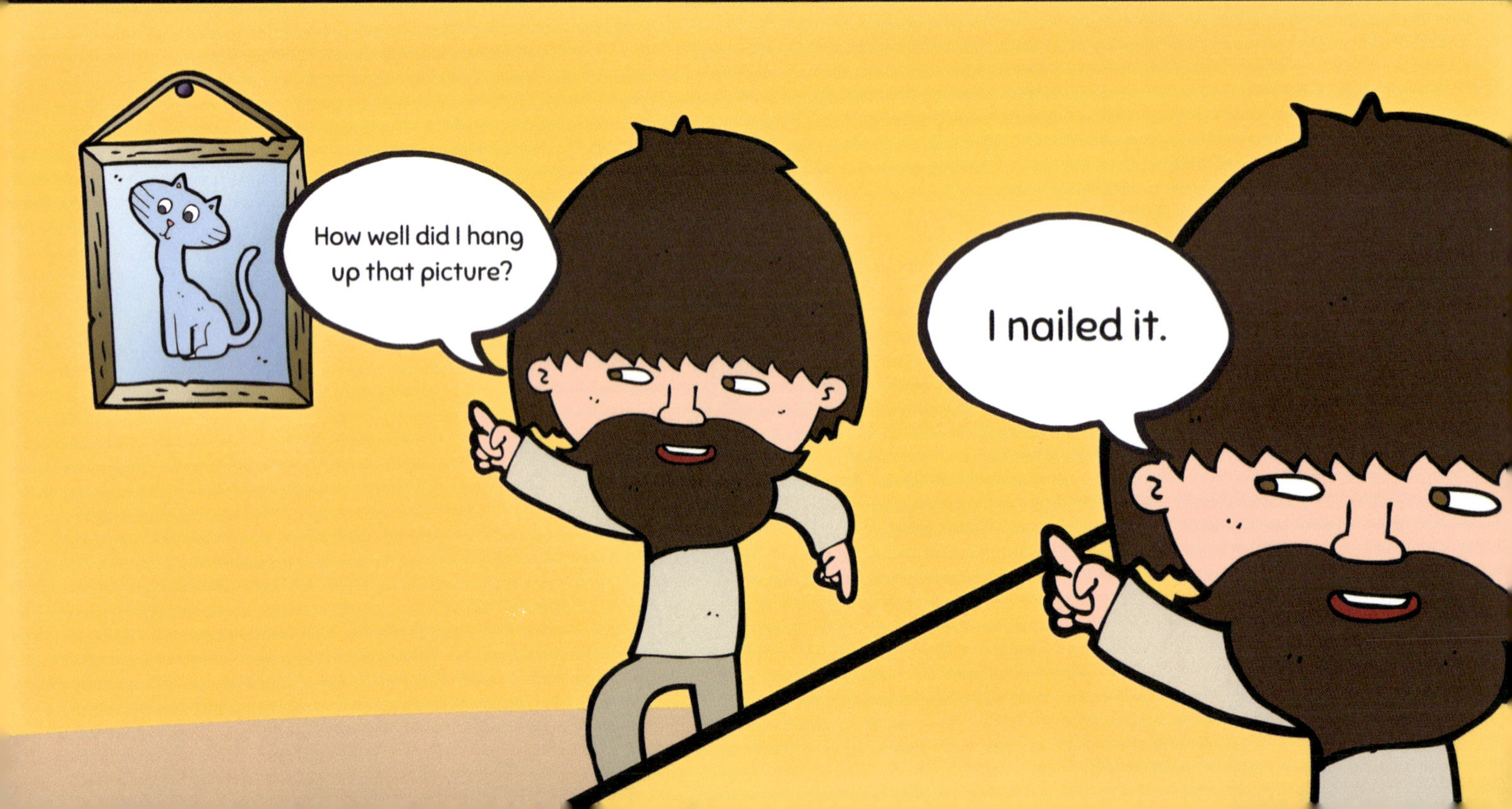

Knock, knock.

Who's there?

Ivan.

Ivan who?

Ivan to know if you enjoyed my jokes? Let me know by leaving a review on amazon.

Follow this link Amazon.com/review/create-review?&asin=B08ZD6TKFP

Or scan below!

Why not collect all the ULTIMATE joke books?

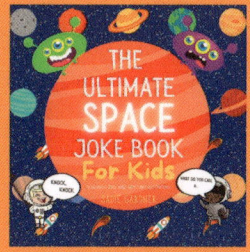
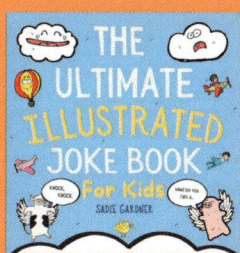
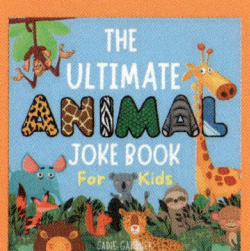

Check them out at

amazon.com/gp/product/B08YM7HM91

Or scan

Printed in Great Britain
by Amazon